Notebook of Last Things

Also by Jon Thompson

POETRY
The Book of the Floating World
Landscape with Light *
Strange Country *

ESSAYS
Fiction, Crime and Empire
After Paradise: Essays on the Fate of American Writing *

(* published by Shearsman Books)

Jon Thompson

Notebook of Last Things

Shearsman Books

First published in the United Kingdom in 2019 by
Shearsman Books
50 Westons Hill Drive
Emersons Green
BRISTOL
BS16 7DF

Shearsman Books Ltd Registered Office
30–31 St. James Place, Mangotsfield, Bristol BS16 9JB
(this address not for correspondence)

www.shearsman.com

ISBN 978-1-84861-648-6

ACKNOWLEDGEMENTS
Thanks to my family for their interest in this book—Suzanne Chester, Zoe Chester-Thompson and Sofie
Chester-Thompson. Thank you, Rae Armantrout, for your endorsement of this book. And to Kelvin
Corcoran, Eric Pankey and Donna Stonecipher: many thanks for generously taking time to read the
book in manuscript form and for offering suggestions for revision. For other forms of support, I am
indebted to Jennifer Atkinson, Barbara Baines, Leigh Deneef, Marc Dudley, Elizabeth Goizueta, Roberto
Goizueta, Nick Halpern, Brenda Hillman, Megan Horstmann, Lew Klatt, Richard Marshall, Leila May,
Jason Miller, Patricia Morgado, Elaine Orr, Don Palmer, Agustín Pasten, Sharon Setzer, Laura Severin,
Claire Thompson, Joe Thompson, Mike Thompson, Sara Thompson, and Chris Tonelli. To Tony Frazer:
thanks for taking this on. And for all you do at Shearsman Books.

And thanks too to the editors of *Artful Dodge, Molly Bloom, Osiris* and *Shearsman* magazine
for publishing sections of this book, sometimes in different form.

Contents

for the unremembered

Come, see real
flowers
of this painful world.
　　　　　　　—Basho

Someone, he added, ought to draw up a catalogue of buildings
listed in order of size, and it would be immediately obvious that
domestic buildings of *less* than normal size — the little cottage in
the fields, the hermitage, the lock-keeper's lodge, the pavilion for
viewing the landscape, the children's bothy in the garden — are
those that offer us at least a semblance of peace, whereas no one
in his right mind could truthfully say that he liked a vast edifice
such as the Palace of Justice on the old Gallows Hill in Brussels. At
the most we gaze at it in wonder, a kind of wonder which in itself
is a form of dawning horror, for somehow we know by instinct
that outsize buildings cast the shadow of their own destruction
before them, and are designed from the first with an eye to their
later existence as ruins.
　　　　　　　—W. G. Sebald, *Austerlitz*

I

1.
The skyscraper across the street
reflects back hundreds of wavy images
of a high-rise hotel, but a blankness where the sky is.

2.
These skyscrapers say, I am the sum
of your vision. Also: I am
monument, surpassing vision.

3.
So many blanknesses. Each with its own
indifference, its own proclamations; its own prayers. The mind
returns to them, again & again, pilgrim without end.

4.
At night a siren starts up, then
another, then others like wolves
driven to keening. Then they slip away.

5.
Haven't seen the rake-thin Vietnamese guy
who wheels his broken bike around as support
for his bowed, badly-set legs, loudly addressing ghosts.

6.
In a stand of trees near some upscale stores they've set
spheres of light high in the branches. Charm or denial,
O brilliant fastidiousness, what we want we keep.

7.
Thought the mentally-ill man downtown
was pan-handling, but all he wanted to do was
bump elbows. Perhaps not even ill.

8.
In the afternoon, light retreats from Nicholson's
Barber & Style with its faded MLK
photo in the window & mint-green sinks inside.

9.
Darkness on the darker Tuscan Cypress, the great
formality of its silhouette a reminder of the graver
virtues, that somber exclamation exceeding architectural time.

10.
Redbrick warehouse district by
the train tracks now warehouses night-clubbers,
art patrons & gourmands.

11.
Lily-white, crimson-red and magenta
azaleas blossoming all along
Dixie Trail, like hypnotic, post-historic prayers.

12.
You want to prove something.
With words, you want to prove
something. As if naming it would do.

13.
Keep seeing the Blue Sky Farms panel truck
round town with its logo
of blue-bordered clouds above rolling green fields.

14.
Memorial in front of the police station:
a dozen or so rough-cut square pillars, different
heights, grouped in Neolithic silence.

15.
Iron-girder skeleton of the new
train station rises up over shining train
tracks curving into the distance.

16.
On Fayetteville Street, smartly-dressed lawyers &
the homeless, shabby in their heavy night-clothes,
mingle freely in the afternoon light.

17.
At the Yellow Dog Bakery, no sign of a
yellow dog, but out front, a young woman suns
her sandal-less feet on a black, wrought-iron chair.

18.
Honda Civic hit a motorcyclist
in five o'clock traffic. Couldn't believe
how high the helmeted body went.

19.
In former tobacco fields they're erecting
faux villages with
chain stores at the street level & condos above.

20.
Trains sounding at midnight
seem to be coming from centuries
back, but the ground-throb's nearer.

21.
Sunlight transparent through
spring leaves, boy I never
was, whirling & dancing, arms out to the sun.

22.
Reader, what is it you
want from this poem? Secret sadness of light?
Unfathomable mystery – or the truth of what you are?

23.
One poet says *We are captives of what we love, what we desire,*
and what we are. Also, & I cannot say if this is said with hope, *An echo*
breaks in us and dies in order for the journey to complete itself.

24.
Bad night last night, the heavens
were violent. Today the world's cleansed, calm,
bright. As if something had ended.

25.
Crescent moon reclining in a bed
of foggy clouds; diffused radiance.
It's the radical non-beauty that startles you.

26.
Big curve of indigo sky & clouds, construction-paper
black, against it. Out walking tonight – finally, cool
air & no regrets, just someone walking alone.

27.
Screeching of the Norfolk
Southern wheels coming to a halt,
hauling chemicals west.

28.

Granite Gothic bell tower & the trenches &
the fallen dead, something now lost
bathed in red lights, surrounded by darkness.

29.

I don't record the things you do,
Recording Angel. No, that's not
true. I don't see the things you do.

30.

Recording Angel, observant companion,
I know you're not interested in poetry, not
even when it breaks all the rules.

31.
I don't record things like you,
Recording Angel. With language, I
peck the eyes out of everything I write about.

32.
In the museum park, the 40-foot cement giant, naked
& headless, sleeps on her side, ankles touching.
Grove of green trees nearby, dreaming.

33.
Life-sized silver tree minus the leaves
rises out of some kind of prairie grass. Shiny, crooked boughs
reach towards an unnaturally blue sky.

34.
Spring breeze can ambush you with its
cold bite, but when blended with the scent of summer, it
gives you a brief, ironic kiss.

35.
To the towering oak with its many-tiered
hierarchy of branches, generations old – to you
I'd bequeath all the smallness in me.

36.
Did I not live/love/fail
all it known, unknown unhindered
by consequence, the earth singing its cyclic song.

37.
Art Deco walkway over the beltline
looks down on six lanes of whizzing traffic.
Chain-link fence to discourage jumpers.

38.
Broken world will break you too. Sometime.
If lucky, you'll feel love. Or
the love of the world for broken things.

39.
So that city the world chooses to forget, city of those who'd
rather be ghosts than living, city that's been destroyed, is
destroyed again. And the Temple that was buried is buried again.

40.
Ghazal of loneliness. This poem's a ghazal of loneliness.
Like the Sahara that stretches on, empty to the horizon.
No, this is a poem about the desert & why we can't do without it.

41.
If we must do these things — what? What
can be adequate to that, that nothing? To the
wind sighing through emptied-out city blocks.

42.
Was reading a poet in 1975 writing about sadness & wondered
if his sadness then was the same as sadness now, or if it had a different heft, ache.
Like different poetic traditions: different, but recognizably poetry.

43.
Sliver-black power lines, then an unlimited
blue like nothing you could ever deserve. With
high, white, self-regarding clouds sailing by.

44.
Birds in the densest greenness singing
a song of songs, call & response, pure song
of the world as home. You must accept it without fear.

45.
Thrashing trees, high winds, air electric. Pause before the total theater
of total power: thunder, lightning, sheeting rain. Two
white lotus blossoms among the wet, shinygreen magnolia leaves.

46.
Through the smoke & dust, the building's bombed-out
wreckage, the Recording Angel sees all the casualties, even the
dusty bodies of the smallest of children. Never notes who does it, or why.

47.
So many words, but no language for
the unseen catastrophe before us, around us.
New words for a new world. Nothing less.

48.
Parking-lot Ferris wheel with lights spoking darkness
makes you see the world from a different angle. Darkness is
childlike, wild & hot. Juggler does unbelievable things, all anti-gravity.

49.
The Edward Jones man keeps knocking
on my door. Today he offered me stock for my "lazy money."
Money, money, money – then the flit into darkness.

50.
Landline used to ring all the time. That
long short-term lease's gone. Now
the black bulky phone's silent, uncommunicative.

51.
Day turns dark. Trees communicate the imminent storm
by telepathy. It's May & mothball-sized hail
is ecumenically punishing roofs, cars & windows.

52.
Prehistoric aspidistras we planted
last fall in the shady patch in the backyard
have brown-edged leaves, burned by winter.

53.
In a sunny patch, the lavender rods resemble
menorahs. Heliotropically following the sun across
the sky, lovely contortionists, only rarely are they upright.

54.
My story I know well, all too well. Review it, daily. But
always, always
the same need for crossing out, revision.

55.
1900: Before "The Preacher" was hanged on Fayetteville Street, he
sold his body to science for $10.00 – for food, iced water
& charity. Even the telephone poles had spectators on them.

56.
Polished granite cobblestones still survive around historic
City Market, though the city has cheated
by wedging cement between them.

57.
Small bronze sculpture of a stylized female figure
wrapped in cloth, her forearm flung in front of her
forehead. Called "Despair," it could also be called "Ecstasy."

58.
At the sleek bank tower downtown, possibilities stretch
to the sky. In the nearby square, they're more down to earth,
constrained by an invisible hand.

59.
Uniformed man at a downtown bus stop at the end of the
day shadow boxes with some shade; bobbing & weaving,
his upper cuts & counter punches come faster & faster.

60.
The world's awash in water tonight. Darkly, darkly.
Drumming, thrumming, thundering down like an intimation
of another life somewhere, not here.

61.
Let us be clear. The cost of not doing anything
is nothing less than the sum
of what shall be & what we shall be.

62.
What to say of failure? It's
never what you think, never
quite the unexpected stranger.

63.
Morning Times's logo: image in the style of
Soviet realism – a worker, shirt sleeves rolled up, holding
up, for heroic veneration, a steaming cup of joe. $2.25 per.

64.
The Recording Angel notes & records but
never speaks. Doesn't say whether
now's the time for the sayable, that sad-faced one.

65.
Is this what we mean when we say hope?
Prefiguration of what's not there, abiding
like a love you never had.

66.
Yes, it will end.
Gesang ist Dasein, Gesang
ist Dasein about nothing, to the end.

67.
Death, it's said, is not
a thing. It's just you
happening in time.

68.
Moonlight filtering through
silence. (Requiem for
Necessity).

69.
It has a secret (distance). Thought's
a train whistle heard in the distance. You
hear it slowly die out, overtaken by silence.

70.
Ghost of a boy walking
on the street at night alone under street lights;
I've seen him many a year.

71.
Rilke says "Every angel is terrifying." But you've seen
his face. The Recording Angel is not terrifying. His
record is.

72.
Remember us, we who spoke the same
words as you, lived the same (un)truths, wanted
the same things as you.

II

1.
Downtown Depression-era lunch counters
& BBQ joints shrink before hermetic
high rises & glass-and-steel skyscrapers.

2.
Talk of drones dropping your latest
purchase from the Fulfillment Center onto
your front door; talk of bug-like drones in war.

3.
Boom boom talk in the night sky.
Wordless, speechless, but *clear*.
Rain like gentle mockery.

4.
At the Gringo-a-Go-Go
talk of Chile & Peru & the Cuban café next
door now doing Cuban & Argentinian food.

5.
Red table umbrellas extended
against the sun. The restaurant: a converted
gas station. Traffic sounds eddy around tables.

6.
A man in dirty stinking clothes totters
in traffic a few yards away. Nothing that
we are, nothing that we're not, redeems it.

7.
Memorial garden for the teacher slain
by her husband at the local school is bordered
by flowers & has a periwinkle bench for reflection, but no plaque.

8.
At the university built by slaves
they just renamed a building first named for
a Reconstruction-era KKK leader.

9.
Violinist for the symphony was
seen cycling with a wounded violin
to the violin repair shop.

10.
Shadow calligraphy wavering on the ground.
Slender branches write Chinese characters for
"paradise" or, perhaps, "death," over & over again.

11.
All movement, no memory, nothing
to add to the nothing that's there, exquisite
dance, in, outside, time.

12.
That sunflower's a text I've tried
to translate, very badly &
incompletely thus far.

13.
Face to the noonday sun, a March breeze
brings down a cloud of white cherry blossoms. Re-
volving in the air, death becomes beauty.

14.
Through all the years, the memory of
the dream he'd had of a teen-age friend, a suicide, sitting
in the branches of a tree saying something inaudible.

21.
The Recording Angel doesn't
listen to the arguments regarding why the innocents
get gunned down. He just tallies the numbers.

22.
"Language should be tortured to tell
the truth." The Recording Angel notes,
indifferently, the need for it & the lies.

23.
You wait & wait for the words
to come to write the poem that will
prove something, that you once existed.

24.
Looking up through the skylight from
my bed, saw white cirrus swirling clockwise
against night thoughts, eye of the universe closing.

25.
Midnight. Under a streetlight, a raccoon
perches on the curb, upright. Waiting. Sickly
smile. Blood trickling from the corner of his mouth.

26.
Noonday pneumatic nail-guns'
contrapuntal rhythms insist
this is the new order now.

27.
Old shotgun houses built
by unsung slaves leveled &
left out by white McMansions.

28.
White "ghost bike" chained to a 35 mph
speed-limit sign on a cut-through between
two busy streets.

29.
I wanted to write a poem about
emptiness. Not emptiness but
emptiness, the kind that fills your life.

30.
Saw workers deconstruct a house today.
Doors, machines, everything that was in was out,
open to the sky. Like a resolution to begin again.

31.
Friday afternoon: dogwood blossoms
playing tag on the empty grey-black
asphalt city parking lot.

32.
Mounds of yellow "Champaign" mangos
from Chiapas in the produce section of the high-end
grocery store look made out of gold.

33.
Be ahead of all parting, as though it were already
behind you, counsels Rilke. Question: can you really live your life like
that? Would you, then, finally, be fully alive?

34.
A few hardwoods next door
support thick cords of ivy
grasping for the crown. Soon they'll cover it.

35.
Words of this poem want so much
to find the right words for the confusion/
hope/pain in my head, but they can't.

36.
On the greenway between the college
& the beltline, bunches of buttercups,
gossiping in the green grass.

37.
Poet posted a photograph of clouds on FB
towering like white headlands over an
Aegean blue. Called it "cloud pornography."

38.
In the old cemetery for the Confederate dead, one
lichened stone for an unknown soldier reads,
"Mother, I have been found. I am home."

39.
And it's spring & sunlight still
tender from being new, laves the day.
And everything is as is if apparent.

40.
And the House of Memory hath no
doors nor roof nor glass windows, its grey Gothic
space a place where breezes come & go.

40.
Inside the House of Memory
plaques commemorate the fallen in some
of the wars; no kind of other remembrance here.

41.
Inscribed on a granite bench in
the House of Memory is the motto, "Tis
the cause, not the fate of the cause."

42.
Outside the House of Memory, on a
slope away from the white sentried tombstones,
young lovers like the wind murmuring in the green grass.

43.
Leaving the cemetery, you can see
rows & rows of headstones
climbing the slope of the hill.

44.
What's the true name of power?
The true name of the powerful:
the true name of the powerless.

45.
And everything to sing for, song
to find the words, joining
in the power of song.

46.
Shadow of the ledger of the Recording
Angel on the floor. O wordless
record, this unreadable tally of catastrophe.

47.
On the front lawn of a house
on Clark, a new semicircle of plastic Adirondack
chairs — salmon pink, lime green, white & fire-engine red.

48.
Mexican carpenters extending the house
down the street play Mariachi music while putting up
2x4s; electricians crank out country music.

49.
Hawk with brocaded white feathers
riding the thermals above
the green soccer fields cares little for sport.

50.
Against a flawless blue sky, the sun's
ravaged disk & in the east, the pale,
crater-pitted moon, like a wan hope, ascending.

51.
One house on Brooks is protected by a small
concrete St. Francis. Next door, miniature pink
flamingos do the honors. The neighbors: an ADT sign.

52.
The Recording Angel records the fresh kills,
the fresh terrors, the fresh ruins in city neighborhoods.
Also in the ledger, all the little-noticed ones.

53.
Things get lost in words, generations gone,
but language travels on, like tinkers
decamping on a cold morning.

54.
Let us be clear. Let us be
clear. The horizon is the horizon
against which we will be measured.

55.
O devout one, take your suicidal wreckage —
the bloodied & obliterated, the broken
& betrayed — as your shining bride.

55.
"The wondrous game that power plays
with all Things." Your shame; your disappointments,
your outsized passions; this world. This life.

57.
And here you are. Late lesson: O world, nothing
instructive in finding you more & more beautiful
& more & more cruel.

III

1.
It's a city of skyscrapers: so much
hidden from view. Mirrors wink in the sun.
Deniability the ultimate principle.

2.
You could claim verticality is about the mirage
of the self & and horizontality is about the mirage of
history. You could claim that.

3.
Walking in the city, everything's hard & durable
— pavement, streets, steel. Why, then, the
insubstantiality, the unreality?

4.
Red & white EMS vehicle parked
in front of the multi-story "Wake County
Detention Center" with flashing emergency lights.

5.
Black man shot by the police had either
four shots in the back or shots in the chest, arms &
shoulder, depending on which autopsy you believe.

6.
Saw the car window wavy with rain. Saw
an empty field in the rain. All normalcy, order,
civilization, berserk in the blurring rain.

7.
Intermittent wailing of security systems outside.
The Recording Angel never finds, or
expects, security. To the contrary.

8.
Used to cars booming music out of
windows; surprised to hear a fleet cyclist using
his lungs as a boom box as he flies down the street.

9.
Small announcement under the larger yellow & green "Jade Garden
Restaurant" sign promises "Under New Ownership," but the light
behind the plastic sign's been out for years now.

10.
In the Odd Fellows Building, circa
1923, the lobby showcases pink-veined marble & brass
art deco sconces. Like the set of a Hollywood film.

11.
Old man, bald black head down, sitting in front
of an abandoned store singing to himself, not minding
others, the world outside the song he's singing.

12.
Street cowboy walking around with pointy
cowboy boots w/ bandanas dangling down. Leather jacketed,
he's equipped with a smart phone & a backpack.

13.
Decaying Velvet Cloak Inn with its ornate,
French Quarter wrought-iron balconies: ode to
corruption. All the stately auxiliaries to the status quo.

14.
New brushed-nickel, aerodynamic
airplane-wing street benches are designed
without backs to discourage extended use.

15.
Startled a black-edged yellow butterfly
on the street. It took off in a jagged, herky-jerky
flight path propelled by fear or joy, I couldn't tell.

16.
At midnight under klieg lights
a ghostly night crew moves around orange cones
before tearing up black asphalt.

17.
Full moon against black velvet
glows with the soft radiance of a
child's plugged-in nightlight.

18.
Last night no sleep. Lying in bed, heard
the 1.15 am train horn cut
the night, pushing darkness ahead of it.

19.
Like crows congregating on high leafless trees,
in the middle of the night, they come back to me, all
the regrets: what I did, what I didn't do.

20.
Wanting a sign that this poem matters. That poetry
matters. That it can survive the moment of its occasion.
Deal is, there's never any such sign.

21.
In this other country I visited I saw
poems, entire poems, written on
the sides of buildings. Like a declaration.

22.
Light loves what's missing, pure
absence, a space it fills with undeniable
grace, ceaseless recuperation of time.

23.
Heat as challenge, the world as lethality.
Desert brought to you, minus the redemption
of mountains. But it's not personal. Like all power, it's impersonal.

24.
Heat-wave brightness dazzles
the eye. It pulls oxygen out of the air, your lungs.
No way to be anything else.

25.
Heat slows everything down. Time ticks
down to slow-mo, clockless succession,
everything to be avoided.

26.
Today a cerulean sky isolates
some odd cumuli in a frieze of menacing
beauty, the entrapment working to a remorseless end.

27.
At the Farmer's Market, long tables full of baskets of
Freestones, Clingstones, Red Tops
& Elegant Ladies. Also, as accents, piles of orange zucchini.

28.
You need strength to face summer, season of
greatest repetition, betrayals of the sun, you
versus the past on display.

29.
O Fourth of July, O heat O picnics & fireworks
popping & bursting the black dome, when
is too much of a virtue too much?

30.
Distracted by sun-stricken streets with
a sound-muffling AC, I half hear a report
of a drone that killed someone important somewhere.

31.
Felt in the emptiness of an afternoon
an odd pain in my chest
where I thought my heart should be.

32.
In this poem, there's so much wreckage.
The alias of language points to it & you see it
or maybe not. It's a question of what can be seen, borne.

33.
Mixed vinegar, saltpeter & orange oil
in a lethal batch to kill weeds. Today,
death smells like citrus in blossom.

34.
In a high-ceilinged church with bare walls, an unearthly
light falls through tall Calvinistic windows onto
a crowded funeral service, "O what needless pain we bear."

35.
But to listen, just to listen. And then
to feel & not to translate it into the single thing you want
so much, going along as if there was world enough & time.

36.
Fat spear-headed lemon balm leaf, juniper green,
promises hope, that the day might yet be
wholesome, aromatic, refreshing.

37.
The Recording Angel feels *what*
as he records us? Infinite compassion? Pity?
Disgust? Or utter indifference? The record does not say.

38.
So much silence in between
the words. So much unsaid in the said.
Like a promise you're not sure you want fulfilled.

39.
This poem resists my dissatisfaction. Despite
the fact that it's damaged beyond recognition, it
doesn't want me to acknowledge any failure, any wounds.

40.
Say, who said the rules are thus
& so? Who said? That so many work so much
every day for so little. Who said?

41.
The Recording Angel can't record all
the daily, lived inequalities, the casual, unseen
wreckage. The general annihilation of hope.

42.
I dreamt of blood, blood running down streets &
of people running & of handwriting that ran down the page, but
when I woke I couldn't find the connections.

43.
Unspoken prayer: start from nothing
& find the pavane silence, hear in it the
nothing-more-to-say, nothing's inexplicable grace.

44.
Burgundy-red Crimson Fire we planted throbbing
with darkness. Grounded, that fierce blood scorns
the over-refined performance of flowers.

45.
Sweet perfume of honeysuckle; walking
through a pine forest a lifetime ago
I remember the air abuzz with it.

46.
When traffic backs up on the interstate at
six p.m., the snake-like line of
cars looks like it's fleeing a catastrophe.

47.
Hawks circle the thermals above
black highways cut through pine forests waiting
for roadkill.

48.
Nicaraguan black beans bubbling
in a pot with orange carrots, green celery, white
onions along with aromatic herbes de Provence.

49.
Like the observant angels in Renaissance paintings,
the Recording Angel is to be found in
an adjacent room or unnoticed corner, half here.

50.
Woke up to the growling of weed-eaters
next door. Just to be here, on an ordinary morning,
caught in that narcotic rhythm, with no thought of woe.

51.
Every second Thursday trashcans line the street
with an overabundance of summer — half-dead branches,
leaves & vines overflowing like abandoned thoughts.

52.
Swelter of August heat & humidity
makes just doing the tour of Stagville
Plantation an effort.

53.
You can see it. It lives in two
eras at once. The tragedy that neither
recognizes the other hangs heavy in the air.

54.
From the main house, the rippled
glass windows upstairs looked onto tended
fields, now reclaimed by trees.

55.
What elegant writing desks, what elegant language, what
fine quill-scratched scripts
did to make a black-and-white world.

56.
The home-made red brick
in the chimney of the slave house
bears the toe prints of a baby, now many years dead.

57.
Its silver-grey board and batten exterior
two stories high, flanked by chimneys, announces
no secrets. Surviving among a spreading quietness & shade.

58.
All the voices crying out that never
get heard. All the voices crying out that get heard & nothing else.
The sun's our utopia. Why can't we accept that; here, now?

59.
Let us be clear. We don't want
clarity about what we've done.
The toy, forgiveness, is what we want.

60.
Say, is it true the dead devour
the living? That the world is ruin, that
we exist only to nourish the past? Recording Angel, tell me.

61.
Late afternoon cicada chorus rises & falls, rises
& falls, vibrating through the humidity, song
of a new generation intent upon itself.

62.
Down the road, the steady hum of
the new house's AC unit is drowned out
by their swelling song.

63.
Cloudless grey sky today. The
emptiness of an ordinary Sunday zeros
out everything else.

64.
Whose god rules over
the life you live? Yours
or someone else's?

65.
Don't look into night, into darkness, densest
blackness, for forgiveness. It's
not there.

66.
From the small speaker on my shelf come voices
thinned by unthinkable suffering; at other times, voices
of unthinkable beauty erase the known world.

67.
What of the innermost whir of the daily? Sometimes you
can almost hear it. Other
times, it's just mental flim-flam, relentlessly overdubbed.

68.
Let's be clear. That ordinary tree's metropolis
of leaves, dancing in sunlight, multiplies with a
casual cosmopolitanism & no fear of strife.

69.
In this city of oaks, thick roots buckle
sidewalks, forcing concrete slabs to tilt
against each other with unplanned abandon.

70.
In the local super-clean, super-bright, supermarket
a sign next to the shopping carts announces free
99.9% hypoallergenic, anti-bacterial wipes for your cart.

71.
In case you misread its sign, the Trophy Brewing
Company erected a life-size
corrugated aluminum beer vat out in front.

72.
Can't help it; every day I check an app
on my phone to see
what I'm worth.

73.
Let's be clear. To live with
fear — Fear — & to accept it as Law
is to live in the despot's country.

74.
To become a foreigner in your own land. That's
what it means to travel in this way, over empty fields. Until
you no longer remember the words that made you you.

75.
I want to say that the present can
redeem the past, that the power exists to heal
the grievous histories. I want to say that.

76.
The Recording Angel does his work
silently, quill on ledger, himself
& the big book voiceless in a voiceless world.

77.
And what of possibility? At any moment, I/you/this poem
might burst into another being, dying for the last time
in a life that shouldn't have been.

78.
In the painting, you can't tell what's present, what's
past; what's a dream, what's not. Everything
that is/was/imagined/forgotten floats in blue's tender embrace.

Notes

These poems refer to, and talk back to, a number of poets and writers — Basho, Walter Benjamin, Paul Celan, George Oppen, Mahmoud Darwish, Jorge Luis Borges, Wallace Stevens, Franz Wright, W.G. Sebald, Osip Mandelstam and Rainer Maria Rilke. In writing this book I've come to think of poems as letters passed between the living and the dead.

"Language should be tortured to tell the truth" is a line from the essay "The Poetic Torture-House of Language" by Slavoj Žižek.

I owe a debt to Harryette Mullen's *Urban Tumbleweed* for suggesting the possibilities in arranging short lyrics, composed in serial fashion, to evoke different dimensions of urban life.

I owe another kind of debt to the work of Marc Chagall, which mixes the ordinary and extraordinary in fantastic, visionary ways. His immanent/transcendent paintings neither flee from the history that created them, nor are they defeated by it.

Lightning Source UK Ltd.
Milton Keynes UK
UKHW050654070319
338578UK00001B/5/P